Going Forth as a Missionary Disciple

Deacon Mark Krejci, PhD

Nihil obstat: Rev. Xavier Ilango, STL PhD
Censor Librorum
June, 23, 2022

All rights reserved. No part of this book may be reproduced, stored in a retrieval system, or transmitted, in any form or by any means, electronic, mechanical, photocopying, or otherwise, without the written permission of Mark Krejci.

The scripture quotations contained herein are from the New Revised Standard Version: Catholic Edition. Copyright © 1989 and 1993, by the Division of Christian Education of the National Council of the Churches of Christ in the United States of America. Used by permission.
All rights reserved.

The logo on the front and back cover is meant to symbolize the priest elevating the Body of Christ during the Mass as well as the faithful going out of the doors of the church to bring the light of Christ to the world.

The Diocese of Crookston
www.crookston.org

Copyright © 2022 by Mark Krejci

TABLE OF CONTENTS

Part 1: Called to be a Missionary Disciple . 1

Chapter 1: *Disciples Wanted: The "Job Description" of a Missionary* Disciple 5

Chapter 2: *This Statement is Meant for All Catholics: You Are a Priest* 11

Chapter 3: *Living as a Prophet One Little Story at a Time* 18

Chapter 4: *You Have a Royal Mission* . . 25

Part 2: Living as a Missionary Disciple. . 32

Chapter 5: *All Ministry is Grounded in Prayer.* . 34

Chapter 6: *Do You Choose "A" or "B" as a Missionary Disciple of Jesus?*. . . . 42

Chapter 7: *Prepare Yourself to Share Beauty, Goodness, and Truth* 50

Chapter 8: *Art of Accompaniment: Pope Francis Wants Me to be an Artist?* 58

Chapter 9: *You Haven't Been Given a Job, You've Been Called to Ministry* . . . 66

Chapter 10: *Jesus Has Jumped Into Your Boat: Do Not be Afraid* 73

Appendix A: Additional Resources . . . 83
Appendix B: Options for Missionary Disciples. . 85
Appendix C: Missionary Ministry Outline . . 91

Part 1

Called to be a Missionary Disciple

I wrote this book to serve as a guide to help you answer the important question: What does it mean to be a missionary disciple of Jesus Christ? Jesus tells us: *"Go into all the world and proclaim the good news to the whole creation"* (Mk 16:15). This call is echoed in the New Testament, found in the writings of the Church Fathers, and repeated by popes, priests, religious, catechists, and others across the history of the Church.

It is likely that every Catholic reading this book knows at least one person who has left the Church. We have all noticed that, over the previous decades, fewer people are attending Mass or coming to the Church for other Sacraments. This has reflected an overall decrease in the United States in religious belief and participation in a parish or congregation. Young adults have the lowest levels of belief in God and religious worship participation that we have ever seen in this country, leading them to be labeled: "the least religious generation in US history."[1]

Pope Francis wants YOU to do something about this. He published *The Joy of the Gospel* early in his pontificate as a call to all Catholics to live as missionary disciples of Jesus Christ, and share the Good News of the Gospel with everyone we meet.

This mission is meant to be a "new evangelization" of the Gospel, which was called for by Vatican II, St. Pope Paul VI, St. Pope John Paul II, and Pope Benedict, along with many others in the Church. Before he retired, Pope Benedict assembled an international gathering of bishops (called a synod) to discuss how the Church should launch the new evangelization around the world. After a synod, the Holy Father writes an "apostolic exhortation" on the synod's topic, but Benedict retired, and so it fell to Pope Francis to write the exhortation.

He selected the title *The Joy of the Gospel* to communicate that, "an evangelizer must never look like someone who has just come back from a funeral!"[2]

We are to be filled with great joy as we share the Good News of Jesus Christ. Pope Francis wrote that we are **all** called to share the joy of the Gospel:

---

[1] Twenge, 2017, p. 128
[2] *Evangelii Gaudium (Joy of the Gospel)*, 10

> "In virtue of their baptism, all the members of the People of God have become **missionary disciples.**"[3]

and

> "Every Christian is a missionary . . . We no longer say that we are 'disciples' and 'missionaries,' but rather we are always **'missionary disciples.'**"[4]

Finally, Pope Francis calls for our missionary ministry to be at the center of our life:

> "I dream of a 'missionary option,' that is, a missionary impulse capable of transforming everything, ..."[5]

This book will help you understand how you can have a "missionary impulse" at the center of your life. The first part will explain what it means to be a missionary disciple, and the second part will describe some steps to take to live as a missionary disciple. Of course, everything about serving as a missionary disciple of Jesus Christ cannot be covered in one book, unless we are talking about the Bible! Consider this

---

[3] *Joy of the Gospel*, 120
[4] Ibid
[5] Ibid, 27

book to be one approach to responding to Pope Francis's call from *The Joy of the Gospel* that we live as missionary disciples of Jesus Christ, responding to our Lord who calls on us to, "Go into all the world and proclaim the good news to the whole creation" (Mk 16:15).

Chapter 1
~
Disciples Wanted: The "Job Description" of a Missionary Disciple

My wife once went to a local "fast food" place for a taco salad, but when she tried to enter, there was a sign indicating that, due to a shortage of workers, she had to order online and then drive up to the window when she received a message that her order was complete. In front of the business was a sign that read "Help Wanted: Immediate Job Offers Available!"

In the Gospels, we hear a "job offer" from Jesus: "Go into the whole world and proclaim the Gospel to every creature" (Mk 16:15). You could say we all applied for this "job" at our baptism. Pope Francis, in the *Joy of the Gospel,* wrote, "In virtue of their baptism, all the members of the People of God have become missionary disciples."[6] Thus, you have been "offered

---

[6] *Joy of the Gospel,* 120

the job," or really given the vocation and ministry, of being a missionary disciple of Jesus Christ.

When I give presentations about our call to be missionary disciples, people often ask a very practical question: What does this mean for my life? One Catholic, who I will call "Teresa," put it something like this:

Teresa: "What does it mean for **ME** to be a missionary disciple of Jesus Christ? Could you give me a 'job description?'"

Deacon Mark: "Well, the complete job description is found in the Gospels and the Catechism of the Catholic Church."

Teresa: "Is there anything shorter?"

Deacon Mark: "What about reading Pope Francis's *Joy of the Gospel?*"

Teresa: "No thanks, just give it to me in one sentence. What does it mean to be a missionary disciple?"

Deacon Mark: "Well, Teresa, you are to pray, discern, and prepare in order to live as a priest, prophet, and king and accompany others as they grow in their relationship with Jesus and his Church."

Teresa: "Huh? What does that mean?"

Deacon Mark: "I know; it's tough trying to capture the Gospel, the Catechism, and the two thousand plus years of tradition in one sentence!"

While I suggest that the "one sentence" I gave to Teresa can serve as a basic guide, this book seeks to provide a deeper reflection about how to live as a missionary disciple. You will find in Holy Scripture and the tradition of the Church[7] that all followers of Christ are called to be "priest, prophet, and king"[8] as we live the Christian life. To do this, we need to center our lives in the Mass and spend time in other forms of prayer as we continue to discern God's call and prepare ourselves to share the Good News in the world. We do this to practice what Pope Francis calls the "art of accompaniment," serving as a spiritual friend and guide to others as they become closer to Jesus.

In the Gospels and throughout the history of the Church, Jesus has posted a "Help Wanted" sign for missionary disciples, and we were all "hired" at our baptism. Even though it is overly simplified, you could say that the "job description" of a missionary disciple looks something like this:

---

[7] e.g., the rite for Baptism, and from the documents of the Second Vatican Council: *Lumen Gentium, Apostolicam Actuositatem*
[8] I will be explaining each of these in the next chapters.

Wanted: Missionary Disciples
Job Description: Live as a priest, prophet, and king, reflecting the Love of Jesus Christ in the world.
Job Duties: Pray, discern, and prepare to accompany others into a closer relationship with Jesus.

In the following chapters, you will read about the different elements of the "ministry description" (I like this phrase better than "job description") for a missionary disciple of Jesus Christ. If you have been baptized, you entered this ministry. And just think of the "compensation" you receive: love and peace in the world and the joy of heaven in the life to come.

Prayer

Jesus Christ, you send your disciples on mission to make God's love and mercy known. Pour out your Holy Spirit upon me so that I may go forth as your missionary disciple, reflecting God's love in the world and speaking your name to others. May my life as a missionary disciple bear fruit in my community and parish as I seek to accompany others toward You and Your Church. Who live and reign with God the Father, in the unity of the Holy Spirit, God forever and ever.
Amen.

Going Forth As Disciples Prayer
Diocese of Crookston

Reflection Questions

I offer these questions at the end of every chapter to provide a time of personal reflection or for group discussion.

1. What is one Gospel passage that you especially like or that touches you in some way?

2. Who is one person who has reflected the love and shared the name of Jesus with you? It might be someone who was or is regularly a part of your life, or it could be someone who had a brief impact on your life in the past.

3. As you begin to read this book, how would you answer Teresa's question: What does it mean for YOU to live as a missionary disciple of Jesus Christ?

Chapter 2
~
This Statement Is Meant for All Catholics: You Are a Priest

When I was a young kid, I would serve morning Mass in the summer. The 6:45 a.m. Mass was held on weekdays, and when I was assigned to serve, I would get up early and ride my bike across East Grand Forks. Sometimes, my hands got so cold in the early morning chill that I had to have one warming in my pocket while the other steered, switching back and forth before frostbite set in!

I would arrive at Sacred Heart and prepare to serve while a priest would be setting things up. I enjoyed my interactions with all the priests, but a unique memory of one priest stands out: his "holy presence." Fr. Larry Wieseler, now retired, was a young associate at Sacred Heart when he made an impression on me that not only shaped me as a kid but also continues to impact me today.

He was never my pastor; I believe I have only spoken with him briefly a few times over my adult life, and I have never attended a Mass when he presided since my elementary school years at Sacred Heart (Fr. Wieseler served most of his priesthood as a missionary in Venezuela). But even though he was a priest in my life for only a brief period, I will always remember him.

The impact he made on my life is not based on anything he said. (Sorry, Father, but none of your homilies or our conversations remain in my memory). Rather, what impacted me is what I like to call his "holy presence" in the sacristy and when he was presiding at Mass. I remember thinking that if I was going to be a priest one day (and what Catholic school boy didn't at least consider becoming a priest?), I wanted to be a priest like Fr. Wieseler.

Most of the people who will read this book are not ordained priests, but we are all called to be priests, for we all share in the priesthood of Jesus Christ. I ask you to consider this important question: how can we all become a priest like Fr. Wieseler, reflecting a "holy presence" in the world?

In the previous chapter, I presented the "job description" of a missionary disciple, and I introduced the idea that we are each called to be priest, prophet, and king. When we are baptized, during the anointing with the sacred Chrism, the priest or deacon says, "He (God) now anoints you with the Chrism of salvation, so that you may remain as a member of Christ, Priest,

Prophet, and King, unto eternal life." As Christians, we are called to live these three roles, or what the Church calls the three "offices," of our discipleship.

In our priestly role as missionary disciples, we are to "bear witness to Christ,"[9] or as Bishop Robert Barron wrote, "A priest fosters holiness, precisely in the measure that he or she serves as a bridge between God and human beings."[10] Notice that Bishop Barron uses "he or she" to emphasize that all Catholics are to live as priests; that we are all called to foster holiness in the world.

There are many ways to foster holiness in the world. The document *Lumen Gentium* from Vatican II teaches that we foster holiness by the way we live our life, by the way we engage in prayer and the sacraments, in how we give glory and praise to God, and by how we act with charity toward others. We are called to be grounded in the Mass and other forms of prayer so that we are prepared to reflect the Love of God in the world.

As you consider how to grow in your priestly role as a missionary disciple, think about the guidance from *Lumen Gentium*. You should go to Mass every Sunday and try to go to Mass more often. And when you go to Mass, fully participate with joy. Next, consider how you pray in your daily life. As a baseline, Catholics

---

[9] *Lumen Gentium (Light of the Nations),* 10
[10] Barron, 2014

should pray every day, thanking God for blessings and lifting up struggles. We should pray for our friends and family, for those we like, and for those we may not get along with very well. Over the course of our day, we should live lives that reflect joy in the world. We should seek to participate in acts of charity, be helpful to others, and do acts of kindness. By making a gift of your life to others, you imitate Jesus, who gave his life as a gift for us on the Cross.

As missionary disciples, we should be a "holy presence," a "priestly presence," in the world. As you strive to fulfill the priestly role of a missionary disciple, you may never know what you will do that will make a holy impact. I bet if you asked Fr. Wieseler the question, "What did you do or say that impacted Mark Krejci so deeply when he was that grade school kid serving Mass?" he might reply, "I have no idea." Or he might even say, "I don't even remember him serving."

I would not be surprised if he said something like that because, as I indicated earlier in this chapter, I also cannot precisely tell you much about those early mornings over fifty years ago. But isn't this the joy and wonder that comes from serving as a missionary disciple of Jesus? You just never know how or when the Lord is going to use you to be a holy presence in the lives of others.

While Fr. Wieseler responded to God's call to live as a missionary disciple by moving to another country, you are likely not called to do the same. For most people reading this book, you are called to live a priestly presence in your community, in your parish, and in your family. May you live your priestly role by growing as his disciple and reflecting the Love of God so that, as I say about Fr. Wieseler, people will say that you reflect a "holy presence" in the world.

Prayer

Come Holy Spirit, fill the hearts of your faithful and kindle in them the fire of your love.

Send forth your spirit and they shall be created. And you will renew the face of the earth.

O God, who by the light of the Holy Spirit, did instruct the hearts of the faithful, grant that by the same Holy Spirit we may be truly wise and ever enjoy his consolations.

Through Christ our Lord,
Amen

Prayer to the Holy Spirit

Reflection Questions

1. Who has reflected a "holy presence" to you?

2. How can Catholics "foster holiness" and serve as a "bridge between God and human beings"?

3. How do <u>you</u> "foster holiness" and serve as a "bridge between God and human beings"?

4. How does your prayer life prepare you to "reflect the Love of God in the world"?

Chapter 3
~
Living as a Prophet One Little Story at a Time

Every August, a friend of mine makes his yearly "prophecy." When asked, "How do you think the Minnesota Vikings will do this year?" his prediction is always, "They are going to win the Super Bowl!" If you follow Vikings football, you know that he is not a very good prophet—his prediction has never come true. But every year, he makes the same claim with enthusiasm. If the Vikings ever win the Super Bowl in his lifetime, will we call him a prophet? No, we will simply say that if you keep making the same prediction, it is bound to be right at some point (well, maybe not about the Vikings winning the Super Bowl).

When we think of prophets in Sacred Scripture or in the life of the Church, we should not think about making predictions about the future. After all, the Greek word "prothitis" means "one who speaks for another." You see, prophets are people who speak on behalf of God.

In the previous chapters, you learnhed that we are all called to imitate Christ and be "priest, prophet, and kings" As a priest, you are to bring a "holy presence" to the world. In this chapter, I will discuss what it means for you to be a "prophet," or, to use the Greek definition, a "spokesperson for God."

Allow me to begin with two examples. Once, on the same day, I had two people act as prophets in my life. These two women shared a bit of their faith story with me, and each said something that continues to help me better understand how all Catholics can follow Christ and live as prophets. I believe the Holy Spirit sent these two into my life to help me better understand what it means to be a prophet and a missionary disciple of Jesus Christ. What prophetic words did they share with me? Let me set the scene.

A group of us were talking about why many Catholics are hesitant to share their faith story and why some never develop a desire to do so. As missionary disciples of Jesus, it is important for us to share our faith story, but during the conversation, we reviewed data indicating that Catholics do not share their personal faith story very often. I ended by proposing to those gathered that they should seek to share their faith story with others and thus serve as models of how to share the story of Jesus with others.

After the meeting, one of the "prophets" asked me, "What do you mean by 'my faith story?' I don't have **A** faith story but **MANY** stories about my faith." She explained that it is intimidating to be asked to share her entire faith story, but that it is much easier to share one or two "little" faith stories. She went on to describe one of these stories, about the time her friend suggested to her that she should read the Bible every day. She told me that she acted on that suggestion and doing so changed her life. She grew to love daily reflections on Holy Scripture and does this every day. Wow, what a great "little" faith story to share with others. I thanked her for being a prophet to me in that conversation by freely sharing one small part of her relationship with Jesus.

The other prophet sent me an email after the meeting in which she wrote that she has never shared her "faith story" with others, but she does offer to pray with and for other people. This is wonderful. Her prophetic mission is not to share with others a specific story about her faith, but by asking people if they want to pray, she is living her faith story. She is letting people know that she is a person of prayer and also believes in the power of prayer. By asking others, *Do you want to pray?* she is sharing her faith story.

If you read the beginning of this chapter and thought to yourself, *I'm not a prophet*, or *I don't know how to speak for Christ*, remember that being a prophet does not mean you have to share the entire Gospel. You do not need to be the source of new revelation. You do not have to have a long and elaborate faith testimony. Rather, as a prophet of Jesus Christ, be ready to speak the name of Jesus to others and talk about how he and his Church have touched your life. Just think what would happen in your hometown if every Catholic would share some of the following with others over the course of a week:

- "I love the Mass."
- "I will pray for you."
- "Have you thought about reading the Bible?"
- "Father had a great Homily this past Sunday."
- "Would you like to come to our parish block party?"
- "I find peace in Jesus."
- "I love receiving the Eucharist at Sunday Mass."
- "The Catholic Church is a great home."
- "I don't know what I would do without my faith life."
- "Yes, I'm a Catholic."

Think of these as prophetic statements, words of a prophet talking about Jesus Christ and his Church. When you think of prophets, you might picture the biblical authors, such as Isaiah, Jeremiah, Paul, or John. You might also think of great Catholic Saints, such as St. Therese of Lisieux, St. Teresa of Avila, or St.

Catherine of Siena. My brothers and sisters, make sure you also think of yourself as a prophet. Rather than great works of biblical or saintly writing, you are prophets called to share your faith with others, one little story at a time.

Prayer

I am created to do something or to be something for which no one else is created;
I have a place in God's counsels, in God's world, which no one else has;
whether I be rich or poor, despised or esteemed by others,
God knows me and calls me by my name.
God has created me to do Him some definite service;
He has committed some work to me which He has not committed to another.
Amen

St. John Henry Newman

Reflection Questions

1. What are two favorite stories about your faith? Are they stories about God, Jesus, the Holy Spirit, or one of the Saints? Or do your favorite stories include something about the Catholic Church or about your parish, or a memory from the past?

2. How do you share your faith story through the way you live your life?

3. When did someone share a faith story with you that helped you grow in your faith? Have you shared a story with someone else, and how did that go?

4. What keeps Catholics from freely sharing their faith? What prevents you from sharing your "little" faith stories?

Chapter 4
~
You Have a Royal Mission

As I sat down to write this chapter, a series of TV commercials from many years ago for a product called "Imperial Margarine" came to mind. Someone in the commercial would put the margarine on a piece of bread or corn on the cob and take a bite. You would then hear a trumpet flourish and see a royal crown appear on their head. The Imperial Margarine company was trying to give people the message that, by eating this margarine, people would feel like they were royalty.

We were given a royal mission through our baptism. You may recall that I have already shared how, at baptism, the newly baptized Christian's head is anointed with the sacred Chrism, and the priest or deacon says, "He now anoints you with the Chrism of salvation so that you may remain as a member of Christ, Priest, Prophet, and **King**, unto eternal life."

The previous two chapters looked at being a "priest" and "prophet," and so, as I expect you figured out by now, this chapter will look at our "kingly" or "royal" office in Jesus Christ. In their own way, all of the People of God are "made sharers in the priestly, prophetical, and kingly functions of Christ."[11] So, this chapter will look at what it means to be called to the "sacred duty of a king."

Let me first address one thing—I am going to use the word "king" because this word is used in the Bible and the documents of the Church. I will not be using king/queen, but remember that both men and women are called to share in the "royal office" of Jesus Christ.

And what is this office, this sacred role we play in the world? Keep in mind that many countries and peoples believed, over many centuries, in something known as the "divine right of kings." This meant that the king had been ordained by God to lead the kingdom. This did not mean that the king had power to do whatever he wanted. On the contrary, the "divine right" had more to do with responsibility than power. The king or queen in the Christian world was meant to organize their kingdom in the way that God intended.

Royalty were meant to use the office that God gave them to bring about the Kingdom of God in their kingdom. Some kings and queens did this in such an extraordinary and holy way that they are recognized as saints. As someone with Czech ancestry, when I think of royalty who sought to follow God's law, I have a

---

[11] *Lumen Gentium*, 31

special fondness for St. Wenceslaus, who is associated with the Christmas carol "*Good King Wenceslas*".

Your royal office, your sharing in the Kingship of Christ, means that you are to order your world to Jesus Christ. We are to bring our faith into our work, our friendships, and the way we interact with strangers, so that the world becomes more aligned with the Good News of the Gospel.

This does not mean the place that employs you must be a "Christian business." Rather, you are to bring a "Christian presence" into where you work. You do not have to have only Catholic friends, but you should bring a Catholic understanding of friendship into your relationships with your friends. You do not need to approach every stranger and bless them or pray a rosary with them, but in every stranger, you should see a reflection of Jesus and reflect to them Christ's love through the way you interact with them.

Aligning our world with the Gospel is often done through small statements, gestures, decisions, and acts of love. I know someone who started a business and employs many people of many faiths as well as some with no faith life. But he founded the company with the goal that he would treat every worker with justice and dignity, that the employees were expected to interact in a positive and affirming manner, and that his customers would receive a good product at a just price. He wanted his company to be part of his kingly mission as a Christian.

There are many other examples of how a Christian can align their world to Christ. A public school teacher who understands she cannot talk about her faith in the classroom, can love every one of her students and expect the best out of them because each of her students are created in the image of God. A group of friends who get together for parties AND also make time to get together for prayer. A woman who brings a smile and sense of joy into her interactions with others every day, even though she might be experiencing pain that often accompanies her waking hours.

We are to live lives of service to others, reflecting God's love, truth, and goodness in the world, so that the world is drawn to God. As Fleming Rutledge wrote, "Thus we interpret self-giving actions not so much as examples of individual human moral choices, but as signposts toward God's coming new world, known to us by revelation and promise."[12] In our royal duty, we are to use our lives to align the world with the Kingdom of God.

What do you do? How do you align your daily life in the world to follow your "royal duty" of bringing forth the kingdom of God on Earth? The laity are to bring Jesus into the secular world of their daily lives. They are to "...seek the kingdom of God by engaging

---

[12] Rutledge, 2015, p.357

in temporal affairs (the affairs of society) and by ordering them according to the plan of God."[13]

How did we receive this royal duty? It wasn't by eating Imperial Margarine. It was through our baptism where we were each given the mission of "priest, prophet, and king" as disciples of Jesus Christ.

---

[13] *Lumen Gentium* 31

Prayer

O Lord, guide me to live in unity between my "spiritual" life and "secular" life.

Help me to follow your word in all of life so that I might grow closer to you as I live your word in the world.

May my life in my family, at work, in social relationships, and in my public life help me grow closer to you as I praise you in all areas of my life. You are the vine, and I am a branch, may I bear your fruitfulness in every sphere of my existence and activity.

Amen

St. John Paul II
From Christifideles Laici

Reflection Questions

1. Using St. John Paul II's prayer as a guide, how do you order your world to Christ? In other words, how do you bring a Christian presence to:
    Your family?
    Your work or at school?
    Your social relationships?
    Your public life?

2. Again, using St. John Paul II's prayer as a guide, how do you bring the praise and worship of God to:

    Your family?
    Your work or at school?
    Your social relationships?
    Your public life?

Part 2

Living as a Missionary Disciple

My first job outside of working for my Dad and Grandpa on the farm was at the "Old" Valley Golf Course (the original 9-hole course) in East Grand Forks. I was hired to be a "greenskeeper" at the golf course, and there were three of us in that role. On my first day of work, I knew what my job title was, but I was not sure what I was supposed to do. Jim, my boss, told me that I would have three areas of responsibility: irrigation, mowing the roughs, and maintaining the sand traps.

After Jim listed these three responsibilities, I was still wondering, *But what do I actually do?* Jim sensed I still had questions, so he proceeded to take me around the course and show me how I was to carry out my responsibilities (the old irrigation system was a unique challenge). He taught me well, and I worked at that golf course for six years during high school and college.

In Part 1, I introduced you to your "job description" as a missionary disciple and described that your three "responsibilities" as a missionary disciple are to be a "Priest, Prophet, and King." Perhaps after reading the first chapters, you have the same question I had on my first day of work at the golf course: "But what do I actually do?"

The second part of this book will begin to answer this question. How do we live the three-fold mission of a "Priest, Prophet, and King?" In short, you will read that to be a missionary disciple of Jesus, you pray, discern, and prepare yourself to accompany others into a deeper relationship with Jesus. Part two will begin to cover how to live as a missionary disciple of Jesus Christ.

Chapter 5

All Ministry is Grounded in Prayer

I cannot count the number of times people have asked me, "How long should people pray every day?" I typically respond with this question, "How long do you pray now?" to which I receive a range of answers that are similar to these responses:

A. I don't.

B. My family prays before meals.

C. I pray an Our Father in the morning and a Hail Mary at night.

D. I go to daily Mass; I pray a Rosary every day, read a bit from the Bible every day, and/or I meditate on Sacred Scripture through Lectio Divina.

E. I pray Morning Prayer (and some go on to add) and Evening Prayer.

F. I pray a holy hour (or half-hour) every morning or evening.

G. I pray a holy hour, the Divine Office, typically offer a Mass, often pray the Rosary, and often lead others in prayer.

While it may be obvious that the "G" response comes from a priest, I have received variations of the other responses from Catholics of all ages. I know an older man who prays a Rosary every day for each of his family members. I know another person who spends about thirty minutes per day reading and meditating on the daily Bible readings used in the Mass. I know another lay Catholic who prays the Divine Office, the five prayers that make up the "Liturgy of the Hours."[14] I am sure we all know people in our parishes who go to Mass nearly every day. The list of examples of how much to pray each day can go on and on.

Let me explain why I am beginning this second part of the book by focusing on the importance of prayer. Remember that this section is called "Living As Missionary Disciples," which means you will read about how to be active as a missionary disciple in your life. A key practice for a missionary disciple is prayer.

Prayer is the foundation of the Christian life and for ministry. Without individual prayer, prayer with

---

[14] The five offices of the Liturgy of the Hours are 1. Morning Prayer, 2. Office of Readings, 3. Midday prayer, 4. Evening Prayer, and 5. Night prayer. Priests, deacons, and religious daily pray all or some of these prayers. A growing number of lay Catholics also pray some combination of the above prayers.

others, and, of course, the prayer of the Mass, we will find that our lives as missionary disciples become tiresome and will fade with time. In that case, disciples may become discouraged, self-centered (i.e., thinking that their ministry is simply their actions), or may just give up when times are challenging or no one appears to be responding. You see, without prayer, you are trying to be a missionary disciple all on your own. Without prayer, you think YOU can figure out how to accompany someone else in their relationship with Jesus, rather than allowing the Holy Spirit to use you to accompany someone else in their relationship with God. And so, my brothers and sisters, I invite you to pray that you will be open to the Holy Spirit, who will guide you as a missionary disciple; and I invite you to pray for the missionary ministry of all Catholics, because we are all called to be missionary disciples.

Going back to the variety of answers that I described at the beginning of this chapter, you may wonder, "Which prayer plan should a Catholic who is living as a missionary disciple follow?" I can confidently tell you that you do not want to use option "A"—not praying every day. I have often heard and read that the laity should seek to spend thirty minutes in prayer every day.

For some Catholics, going from saying one prayer per day (e.g., a prayer before supper with the family) to, for example, also praying one decade of the Rosary per day is a big step. For others, moving from praying one Rosary per day to also praying morning and evening prayer is **just** as big of a step.

The growth of your prayer life should not be based on the notion of "my next step," an idea that evokes an image of time or the number of prayers. Rather, I believe the question to ask is this: What is your next **NEED** in your prayer life?

- For those who are seeking to live as a missionary disciple of Jesus, what is your next <u>need</u> in your prayer life?
- For those who wish to deepen their understanding of being a disciple of Jesus Christ, what is your next <u>need</u> in your prayer life?
- For those who have drifted away from God and/or the Church, what is your next <u>need</u> in your prayer life?

The question you should consider is not, "How long should I pray?" but "How do I need to pray?" God is calling you to be in a relationship with Him (to be a disciple), and then go on mission. Prayer is how we keep the relationship with God alive in our daily life, and it is through our prayer that God will guide us on our mission. So, what are your prayer <u>needs</u> right now? I cannot answer that for you except to say, "You need to pray, for prayer is the foundation of the life of a disciple of Jesus Christ; and it is through prayer that

God will reveal to you your mission and sustain you on the journey as a missionary disciple."

Let me suggest to you one prayer resource focused on missionary discipleship. It is a free pdf prayer booklet titled *31 Prayers for Missionary Disciples*. You can use this book to pray one prayer each day of the month, praying that God will guide you and others to spread the love and name of Jesus to the world. You can find this booklet on the Diocese of Crookston web page (www.crookston.org). While on the web page, place your pointer on "Discipleship," and then click on "*Going Forth As Disciples*" on the menu. Scroll down on that page and you will see "31 Prayers," and the booklet will open up for you. I invite you to pray one of these prayers each day; when the month ends, start again on Day 1.

Something to keep in mind about prayer is the need to listen. It is wonderful to recite prayers, to read scripture, or to offer spontaneous prayer to God. But we also need to also listen. One way of organizing your prayer time is using "The Three R's" based on how St. Teresa of Avila taught others to pray. During your prayer time, take time to "Read," "Reflect," and make a "Resolution." Let me break these down:

1. Read: Read Sacred Scripture, one of the prayers from *31 Prayers for Missionary Disciples*, and/or perhaps morning or evening prayer from the *Liturgy of the Hours*. You could also read a book on a spiritual theme. After you have taken time to read, move on to ...

2. Reflect: Take time for silent reflection on what you have read. Which word or phrase runs through your mind? What thoughts, emotions, or images come to mind? What guidance or insight, if any, do you sense from the Holy Spirit? Use this time to listen.

3. Resolution: Decide to do something on this day based on your reading and reflection. Write your resolution on a piece of paper and keep that with you throughout the day. Your daily resolution should be a concrete thing to do that emerges out of your time in prayer.

Prayer guides and fortifies us on our missionary journeys. I encourage you to keep in mind something that Bishop Victor Balke said of prayer: "We just don't understand the mystery of prayer, but we know that God in his goodness will listen to us, respond to us, because he is a good and gracious God."[15]

---

[15] Bishop Victor Balke, 2021, as quoted in *Our Northland Diocese*

Prayer

Christ with me,
Christ before me,
Christ behind me,
Christ in me,
Christ beneath me,
Christ above me,
Christ on my right,
Christ on my left,
Christ when I lie down,
Christ when I sit,
Christ when I stand,
Christ in the heart of everyone who thinks of me,
Christ in the mouth of everyone who speaks of me,
Christ in every eye that sees me,
Christ in every ear that hears me.

St. Patrick

Reflection Questions

1. Look at the list below and identify which prayer practice you do on a daily (D), weekly (W), or on an occasional (O) basis. Next, put an (N) by a few of the options that you believe you "need" more of in your life.

The Mass	The Our Father	The Hail Mary
Table Grace	Rosary or other Marian prayers	Reading the Bible
Chaplet of Divine Mercy	Some or all of the Divine Office	Prayers glorifying God
Eucharistic Adoration	Stations of the Cross	Devotional prayers
Angelus	Lectio Divina	Litanies
Examination of Conscience	Blessing children in your home	Intercessory prayer
The Creed	Divine Praises	Contemplation/ Reflection
A specific set of prayers	A specific time for prayer	A specific amount of time in prayer

2. What is your favorite prayer practice? Which prayer practice do you need to begin? Which prayer practice do you need to develop?

3. Who is someone who has a prayer life you admire? How might you follow their example?

Chapter 6
~
Do You Choose "A" or "B" as a Missionary Disciple of Jesus?

Imagine driving down a rural Minnesota highway in winter, and you find yourself in a snowstorm so thick that you can only see two car-lengths ahead of you. Meanwhile, the road is becoming covered with snow and ice. Of the following options, what would be the best thing to do?

A. slow down

OR

B. speed up

Now imagine that you are walking down a sidewalk or rural lane, and you see a cell phone on the ground. When you pick it up, you see a driver's license in an outside pocket and recognize that this cell phone belongs to one of your neighbors. Of the following options, what would be the best thing to do?

A. return it to your neighbor
OR
B. throw the cellphone into the garbage

One more scenario—say that your employer asked you to complete a task at work by the end of the week. Of the following options, what would be the best thing to do?

A. complete the task on time
OR
B. spend the week on your phone watching goofy videos

The right answers are clear—you should choose "A" in each of the above situations.

As you read each of these scenarios, I suspect you thought, *It's pretty easy to discern which option to follow.* Well, perhaps you did not actually use the word "discern," but think about this word for a bit. The Latin origin for "discern" means to "separate" in the context of separating the good or true choice from the bad or false choice. As Christians, we use this word often within the context of "discerning God's way" or "discerning God's call" for us. So, let me ask you to do some of this discernment right now.

Of the following options, what would God want you to do?

A. love God with all your heart, soul, mind, and strength
OR
B. do not even believe and ignore God

Let me ask you to "discern" one more question. Of the following options, what would God want you to do?

A. love others
OR
B. be mean, vindictive, gossipy, and spiteful to others

The correct answers are clear; you should choose "A" because they are what Jesus teaches us to do (see Mark, 12:28–34).

An important thing to understand about discernment is that the answer is found in God. We live in a culture where many believe that we should each find answers "deep down" within ourselves. This is a self-centered discernment. Christians are called to discern God's truth, God's way, and to live the life God wants for us. Discernment is meant to be finding answers in God – not ourselves.

After reading these scenarios, I hope it was easy for you to discern the God's truth. You are to love God and love people. Of course, in our daily lives, the correct way to do this may not be so easy to see. We are not always given choices as clear as the "A" or "B" options found above. What does it mean to love God every day of our lives? How does this impact the way we live our daily lives? How are we to love everyone we meet? What does it mean to "love the sinner but hate the sin"? How are we supposed to show love for all people?

These are questions that you are called to discern as a disciple of Jesus Christ, but remember that we are NOT discerning these and other questions about the Christian life on our own. In the previous chapter, I wrote about the importance of prayer and that all ministry—ordained, consecrated, and the ministry of the laity—should have prayer as its foundation. Prayer helps us to discern how God wants us to love others and live as missionary disciples of Jesus. In prayer and through prayer, the Holy Spirit will guide us to live as a priest (fostering holiness in others/reflecting a holy presence in the world), prophet (speaking about God, Jesus, the Holy Spirit, and about the Catholic Church), and king (aligning the world to the truth of the Gospel).

Let me have you discern a bit more while you are reading this chapter. Of the following options for living your <u>priestly</u> mission, what does God want you to do?

> A. pray every day and help others grow in their relationship with Jesus

OR
B. occasionally pray and let other people take care of their own relationship with Christ and his Church

Here is another question to consider: of the following options for living your mission as a prophet, what does God want you to do?

A. share one of your faith stories with another person this week
OR
B. never talk about Jesus with other people this week?

Of the following options for living your kingly or royal mission, what does God want you to do?

A. at work or school treat others with respect and dignity so that you reflect the love of Jesus to everyone
OR
B. be mean, cranky, and only take care of yourself or just your "group" at work or school

Again, I hope it is easy to discern that you should choose "A" for each of these.

I hope that God's way is something that you want to follow and that you are able to discern God's call in your life. Discerning how to follow God's way is not always as clear as the scenarios I presented in this chapter. This is why we turn to prayer and Sacred Scripture, follow the guidance of the Church, seek out the guidance of a spiritual friend or mentor, and talk with our family, to help us discern God's call in our lives.

As we discern how God is calling us to be missionary disciples, turn to Jesus, who will show you the way. What is Jesus calling you to do?

>   A. live as his missionary disciple
>   OR
>   B. live a life that rejects this call

The answer is clear—we are all called to discern how to live the "A" option every day of our life.

Prayer

Father,
I abandon myself into your hands;
do with me what you will. Whatever you may do, I
thank you: I am ready for all, I accept all.

Let only your will be done in me, and in all your
creatures—I wish no more than this, O Lord.

Into your hands I commend my soul:
I offer it to you with all the love of my heart,
for I love you, Lord, and so need to give myself, to
surrender myself into your hands without reserve, and
with boundless confidence, for you are my Father.

St. Charles Foucauld,
Prayer of Abandonment

Reflection Questions

1. Appendix B contains several options for missionary action. Of course, being a missionary disciple is more than actions, we also need a "missionary impulse" that elicits our missionary actions. Review the various missionary options found in Appendix B and place a "✓" next to the things you already do and also place a "+" by at least one to three ideas that you may also be called to do.

If you are working on this book in a small group, take time right now to read through Appendix B in silence and consider how God is calling you as a missionary disciple. After people have completed going through the list, share the "+" items from your review.

Chapter 7
~
Prepare Yourself to Share Beauty, Goodness, and Truth

In the previous chapter, you may recall that I presented some choices to discern about God's call in your life. In this chapter, I am going to give you a "pop quiz" to test your understanding of what we believe. To make it easier, this will be a multiple-choice quiz.

1. Who is God the Father?

    A. A mythical being once believed in by primitive people.
    B. A gray-haired old man up in the clouds.
    C. The best thing that has ever been created.
    D. The maker of heaven and earth.

2. What did Jesus do for our salvation?

    A. He was a great teacher like Mohammed or Buddha.

B. He performed magic.
C. He was a man who became most like God.
D. He is the Son of God, who died on the cross, was buried, and rose again, and his kingdom will have no end.

3. Who is the Holy Spirit?

    A. The third person of the Holy Trinity.
    B. Who proceeds from the Father and Son.
    C. Who speaks through the prophets.
    D. All of the above.

4. What is the Catholic Church?

    A. Just like any other religious group.
    B. A denomination that is out of touch with the modern world.
    C. A rule making body trying to take all the fun out of life.
    D. The mystical Body of Christ that is one, holy, catholic, and sent on mission to share the Good News of the Gospel.

5. The final question is a short essay question: What is one thing that you love about being Catholic?

The correct answer to each of the multiple-choice questions is "D," which is not a very creative way to put together a quiz — but it does make self-grading easier.

You may be wondering why I am starting with this pop quiz. While we all became missionary disciples at our baptism, I hear from people that they do not think they can be missionary disciples because they claim they do not know enough about the Church. They tell me, "I don't know enough about the Bible, or the Church, etc. to talk to others about faith." And some say, "Someone might ask me something I don't know or can't explain."

If you think you do not know enough to be a missionary disciple, let me ask you this question: How well did you do on the pop quiz? If you correctly answered these questions, then you do know some core beliefs about Catholicism. And if you were able to answer the "short essay" question, then you have something to share about your personal experience of being a Catholic.

Do you know everything found in the Catechism? You probably don't, and neither do I. But remember that Jesus called the apostles and sent out the seventy disciples before they knew everything about him, and he does the same to us. God sends us on mission, even though we do not know everything about God and the Catholic Church.

You may not completely understand everything, but can you tell people the **truth** that Jesus loves them? Can you share with others the **goodness** that comes through receiving the Body of Christ and being a member of the Church? Can you describe the **beauty** found in the lives of the saints or the image of Christ born in a lowly barn? Are you able to tell others about the Good News that the Church teaches regarding the strength of Christian marriage, the virtues of family life, and the loving care of the poor, the sick, and the people at the margins?

In the previous paragraph, I highlighted the three words that were used in the chapter title: Beauty, Goodness, and Truth. All three are part of God and found in the Church, and others have written that people are attracted to the beauty and the goodness and then wish to know the truth.[16] Are you prepared to share these three with others?

We can all learn more about God, Sacred Scripture, and the Church. Let me encourage you to find an article, watch a Catholic video, look up a topic in the Catechism of the Catholic Church, or ask your parish priest or a catechist for help so that you can learn more about God and the Catholic Church. Just think what the Church would be like if every Catholic learned one new thing about Catholicism each week. And then imagine how you would touch the lives of others if,

---

[16] See the following video from Bishop Barron: "Evangelizing Through the Good" at:
https://www.youtube.com/watch?v=Jv0JN2FWZDM

each week, you prepared yourself to better share the beauty, goodness, and the truth of Catholicism.

Prepare yourself to share one of your faith stories with another person so that, when the Holy Spirit brings someone into your life, tomorrow or later this week or next month, you are ready. Also, prepare yourself by learning more about the faith so that, if someone asks you a question, you may have the answer or know where to find it. Consider reading the Catechism of the Catholic Church, which is, as I heard it recently described, a great love letter between God and the Church. You can read a page or two every day. If not the full Catechism, let me suggest you read the "United States Catholic Catechism for Adults," which presents the Catechism in a way that many find more engaging.[17]

When I encourage people to learn something new about God and the Church, I hear several responses: "I don't like to read," "I don't know where to find things," or "I don't know where to begin." If you do not know where to turn to learn something about God and the Church, Appendix A provides some helpful resources! You can also get involved in adult formation activities in your parish, ask your pastor or another priest, deacon, or a religious sister or brother for

---

[17] You can find information on how to purchase or view this book online in Appendix A.

direction, and/or look through your local or online Catholic bookstore.

Whether you read the Catechism, watch a YouTube video by Bishop Barron, listen to Fr. Mike Schmitz's "Bible in a Year" podcast, read about the lives of the saints, or use the free online Bible Studies offered on the Diocese of Crookston web page, I encourage you to continue to learn something new in order to prepare ourselves to be missionary disciples in the world and to share the beauty, the goodness, and the truth about our Catholic faith.

Prayer

Immaculate Conception, Mary my Mother,
live in me, act in me,
speak in me and through me,
think your thoughts in my mind,
love through my heart,
give me your dispositions and feelings,
teach, lead me and guide me to Jesus,
correct, enlighten and expand my thoughts and
behavior, possess my soul,
take over my entire personality and
life, replace it with yourself,
incline me to constant adoration,
pray in me and through me
let me live in you and keep me in
this union always.

St. Pope John Paul II

Reflection Questions

1. Instead of reflection questions, this section provides a "Reflection Task". Write down five things/topics you wish to learn more about regarding God the Father, Son and/or Holy Spirit, the Bible, the Catholic Church, or Mary and the Saints. If five ideas do not come to you right away, then pray the prayer on the previous page and consider how the various parts of this prayer may call you to learn something more about God and the Church.

    1. _____

    2. _____

    3. _____

    4. _____

    5. _____

2. Where can you go/who can you consult to find out more information about these topics?

Chapter 8
~
Art of Accompaniment: Pope Francis Wants Me to be an Artist?

I cannot even draw a crooked line, let alone one that forms a decent picture. A four-year-old's stick figure drawing of a person is closer to the actual image of a human body than I can produce. When I was in grade school, we were to draw something that we liked to do, and so I drew a picture of a football player; but rather than a running back, my drawing looked more like the Hunchback of Notre Dame. A few years ago, when I was painting with our then three-year-old granddaughter, her use of color and brushstrokes looked like a French impressionist masterpiece compared to my drips of paint on the paper.

What am I to do when I read that Pope Francis wants all Catholics to be engaged in art? Thankfully, he is not talking about the visual, musical, literary, or dramatic arts. Rather, he wants all Catholics to be engaged in the "Art of Accompaniment." He describes the "Art of Accompaniment" as a way for Catholics, as missionary disciples, to "lead others ever closer to God."[18] We are to be spiritual friends and, through our patience and mercy, reflect the Love of God. This "Art of Accompaniment" is to be grounded in the Gospel, and it involves listening with "an openness of heart which makes possible the closeness without which genuine spiritual encounter cannot occur."[19] Accompanying others into a closer relationship with God is to be "steady" and "reassuring," and provide "our compassionate gaze which also heals, liberates, and encourages growth in the Christian life."[20] When you accompany others, you help them connect with God in their daily lives.

Let me move from a definition of accompaniment to offer some concrete examples. I will be brief, but I hope the examples provide a sense of how you can be a spiritual friend to others.

Example #1: Connie and Frank were married in the Catholic Church, but the first seven years were not easy when it came to the Church. Connie's Catholic faith was always central to her life, but Frank remembers that he just "went through the motions" of being a Catholic. He complained about going to Mass, giving to the offertory, and what he called the poor

---

[18] *Joy of the Gospel*, 170
[19] Ibid, 173
[20] Ibid, 169

leadership in the Church (i.e. he regularly complained about every priest that served his parish).

While Connie patiently listened to Frank, she also shared that she loved Mass and received more than what they ever gave to the Church. She also said that she cherished the priests and their ministry; and she believed that, despite the sin amongst its members, the Church was beautiful. Over time, the hardness of Frank's heart toward the Church softened as Connie accompanied Frank into a journey of love with the Mass and the mystical body of Christ. Later in their marriage, Frank regularly and publicly thanked Connie for her patience with him and for the way she showed him what it meant to be a follower of Jesus.

Example #2: When they were in their twenties, Rosita complained to her friend Manuela about having to go to Mass; she would often say, "I do not get anything out of it." One day Manuela said, "Rosita, Mass is not just about you getting something out of it; it's also about what you give to others by being there." They drifted apart over the years, but later on, when they were both in their fifties, Rosita saw Manuela and thanked her for what she said all those years ago. Rosita explained that she kept Manuela's words in her heart and grew to love the Mass. Manuela was stunned; not only did she not remember saying those words about the Mass, but she was also surprised that she even knew what to say back then. Manuela believes it was the Holy Spirit that inspired her words when she was so young. While Manuela's words to Rosita were few, these words accompanied Rosita over many years.

Example #3: John and Francisco were members of the same Catholic parish and worked at the same manufacturing plant. They noticed that Jake always ate lunch alone, others referred to him as an "odd ball," and some of the other workers even picked on him. John and Francisco decided to reach out in friendship. Even though Jake initially seemed reluctant, the three were soon eating their lunches together. Eventually, Jake came along when they went fishing and hunting. As the friendship grew, John and Francisco spoke about the parish and their faith from time to time in the normal flow of conversation, and they found out that Jake knew very little about God and the Church nor was he interested. Yet, after several years, Jake asked them, "Why do you believe in God?" From this question, and over many more years, Jake came to know God and eventually became a Catholic.

Example #4: John and Mary raised their children in the Church. They went to Mass as a family, prayed together in the home, and the children received their sacraments and always went to religious education. As parents, John and Mary understood that they had a responsibility to teach their children about the Catholic faith. However, when their children reached their twenties, they all drifted away from the Church, and some even stated they no longer believed in God. John and Mary were not only hurt by this, but they also wondered, *What did we do wrong?*

They came to realize that their mission of accompanying their children into a deeper relationship with God was not over, and while all their children are not back in Church, all have returned to believing in God. John and Mary told me that they expect that they will be actively accompanying their children until all have returned to the Catholic Church.[21]

While I have changed the names, each of these situations really happened. There are many other examples of accompaniment ministry that I could write about, but I hope that these help you see that there are many ways to be a spiritual friend. You are meant to practice the "Art of Accompaniment" in different ways based on the people and circumstances that arise.

How are you accompanying others closer to God? Remember that accompaniment might occur through what you say to others on one occasion, through sharing a long-term spiritual friendship with others, or through your patient, ongoing witness of the faith. Just as every artist draws a picture in a different way, each missionary disciple will be a spiritual friend to others in their own unique way.

Every Catholic reading this chapter is called to accompany others into a closer relationship with God.

---

[21] John and Mary participated in the *Shepherding Them Home* sessions offered in the Diocese of Crookston.

Who is God sending to you today, this week, this month, this year? God is calling on you to become a spiritual friend to others. May you be blessed with many such people in your life.

Prayer

Lord, you left your Mother in our midst that she might accompany us.

May she take care of us and protect us on our journey, in our hearts, in our faith.

May she make us disciples like herself, missionaries like herself.

May she teach us to go out onto the streets.

May she teach us to step outside ourselves.

May she, by her meekness, and by her peace, show us the way.

Pope Francis
Prayer at the conclusion of
meeting with young people

Reflection Questions

1. Who has accompanied you into a deeper relationship with God? What did they do to serve as your spiritual friend or mentor? Did their accompaniment take place one time, for only a brief time in your life, or have they been with you throughout your life?

2. What is it like to be a spiritual friend to someone else? How have you accompanied others into a closer relationship with God? Have you accompanied others on one occasion, for a brief period, or over for a longer time?

3. Who do you know who needs to see a "compassionate gaze," hear a kind word, or receive a thoughtful gesture from you?

Chapter 9
~
You Haven't Been Given a Job, You've Been Called to Ministry

Don't read the title and think, *I can skip this chapter; it doesn't have to do with me because no one is calling me into ministry!* But imagine if one evening your pastor or bishop called you and said, "I would like you to get involved in ministry." What would you think? *What is this ministry? I don't want to do it—whatever it is. I wonder why he thought of me?* Or you might even ask yourself, *How did bishop get my cell number?*

Or say the Pope called (and you had some way of knowing it really was the Holy Father and not your friend pranking you) and stated, "I need you to get involved in a ministry." What would you think? *Why does the **Pope** want **ME**? How did the Holy Father get my name, let alone my number?* Perhaps you would be in a state of shock!

Some of you may have been called by your pastor or bishop for some type of ministry. I suspect none have been called by the current Pope or any of his predecessors. If you have, let me know, and I will write about the call sometime.

Still, someone has called every Catholic reading this chapter to take on a ministry. The call did not come via your phone but via Sacred Scripture: "Go into all the world and proclaim the good news to the whole creation" (Mk 16:15). Yes, Jesus has called you and this call is as real as if you received a phone call from your priest, your bishop, or the Pope. In the Gospels, when Jesus calls people to the ministry of a missionary disciple, do not think that the words in Sacred Scripture were meant only for those who were directly hearing Jesus. When you read or hear the words of Christ in Scripture, Jesus is talking to you.

I began this book about living as a missionary disciple by using the format of a "Job Description for Missionary Disciples." What I have actually been writing about is the call you have received to the **ministry** of a missionary disciple. As Pope Francis shared in the *Joy of the Gospel*, "In virtue of their baptism, all the members of the People of God have become missionary disciples."[22] Missionary discipleship is part of your ministry as a baptized believer in Jesus Christ and a member of the Catholic Church. This is not a job at which we labor; it is a ministry through which we love.

---

[22] *Joy of the Gospel*, 120

As missionary disciples, we are called to love others by accompanying them toward the Love of God. In the previous chapter, I described accompaniment ministry as being a spiritual friend to others; sharing with them the Good News of Jesus as they seek the Lord. You may be a spiritual friend to someone for years, months, weeks, or even minutes. No matter the length of time, all are called to accompany others toward Christ and his Church.

We are to pray, discern, and prepare so that, when someone comes into our lives, we are ready to be instruments of the Holy Spirit and accompany them on their journey to God. In the previous chapters, you read that when we were baptized, we were anointed "as a member of Christ, Priest, Prophet, and King." As a priest, we are called to a life of prayer, to "bear witness to Christ,"[23] and to serve "as a bridge between God and human beings."[24] As prophet, we are called to talk about Jesus with others, talk about the Good News of the Gospels, and share our faith stories with others. And as king, we are to align the world to Jesus through the way we share the love of Jesus with others: family, friends, people in our community and parish, and those at work or at school.

---

[23] *Lumen Gentium*, 10
[24] Barron, 2014

As part of the *Going Forth As Disciples*[25] ministry in the Diocese of Crookston, I call people (on their phones) from around the diocese and, in various ways, ask them how they are living as priests, prophets, and kings. I have heard wonderful examples of missionary discipleship ministry happening every day in our northwest corner of Minnesota. Catholics are sharing Gospel stories, talking about their faith, inviting people to Mass, encouraging coworkers, supporting adult children who have medical challenges, getting their children to Mass and RE, teaching RE in the parish, bringing food to those who need a good meal, giving rides to the elderly who need medical care, praying with others, advocating for the protection of the unborn, and treating others with respect and fairness.

One Catholic probably even saved a life when she came upon someone who had fallen on the sidewalk in the middle of January; the woman had broken her ankle and leg and had been waiting in the frigid snow for over twenty minutes. This good Catholic woman sprang into action and called an ambulance, and she also comforted the person until help arrived.

It is beautiful to see the many ways Catholics have answered the call to be a missionary disciples. Yet I also know that for others, this seems like a strange or intimidating ministry. If you are wondering, *Am I really supposed to be a missionary disciple?* remember that Jesus

---

[25] The final page contains a description of *Going Forth As Disciples*

has already called you. If you are waiting for an additional call from your priest, bishop, or the Pope before you give it a try, let me know, and I will pass your number along.

Prayer

Dear Jesus, help me to spread your fragrance everywhere I go. Flood my soul with your spirit and life. Penetrate and possess my whole being so utterly that all my life may only be a radiance of yours.

Shine through me and be so in me that every soul I come in contact with may feel your presence in my soul. Let them look up and see no longer me but only Jesus.

Stay with me and then I shall begin to shine as you shine, so to shine as to be a light to others.

Let me praise you in the way you love best by shining on those around me. Let me preach you without preaching, not by words but by my example.

St. John Henry Newman

Reflection Questions

Reflect on these questions as you consider what you have read in this and all the previous chapters.

1. How are you living the ministry of "priest?"

2. How are you living the ministry of "prophet?"

3. How are you living the ministry of "king?"

4. How are you living as a missionary disciple of Jesus?

Chapter 10
~

Jesus Has Jumped Into Your Boat: Do Not be Afraid

I begin this final chapter with a Gospel passage from Luke (5:1–11):

> *While the crowd was pressing in on Jesus and listening to the word of God, he was standing by the Lake of Gennesaret. He saw two boats there alongside the lake; the fishermen had disembarked and were washing their nets. Getting into one of the boats, the one belonging to Simon, he asked him to put out a short distance from the shore. Then he sat down and taught the crowds from the boat.*
>
> *After he had finished speaking, he said to Simon, "Put out into deep water and lower your nets for a catch." Simon said in reply, "Master, we have worked hard all night and*

> have caught nothing, but at your command I will lower the nets." When they had done this, they caught a great number of fish and their nets were tearing. They signaled to their partners in the other boat to come to help them. They came and filled both boats so that the boats were in danger of sinking.
>
> When Simon Peter saw this, he fell at the knees of Jesus and said, "Depart from me, Lord, for I am a sinful man." For astonishment at the catch of fish they had made seized him and all those with him, and likewise James and John, the sons of Zebedee, who were partners of Simon. Jesus said to Simon, "Do not be afraid; from now on you will be catching men." When they brought their boats to the shore, they left everything and followed him.

Jesus has jumped into your boat! Just as he jumped into Peter's boat to send him on his mission (catching people), so has Jesus jumped into your life to call you to your mission as his disciple. Remember how Peter responds to this call from Jesus? When he returned to shore, Peter — along with James and John — left everything. For a Galilean fisherman to leave his boats and nets, his most expensive possessions and his livelihood, was an incredible thing. Note that the passage does not say Peter sold his boat or turned it over to a friend or family member. He just "up and left" everything to begin his mission as a disciple of Jesus Christ.

Peter goes through a transformation in this passage. He starts by responding to the request from Jesus to move into the lake a short distance so that Jesus could preach to the people. Peter listens to Jesus, and then Jesus asks him to do something out of the ordinary. Jesus says to Peter, "Put out into deep water and lower your nets." Remember that Peter was already washing his nets because fishing was done for the day. Peter even tries to tell Jesus that he is tired, has caught nothing, and probably did not expect to catch anything else during the day, yet he still obeys. The net becomes so full of fish that it is breaking, and Peter has to call others (the soon-to-be apostles James and John) for help. After that experience, upon learning that he is to fish for people, Peter leaves everything and begins his mission as a disciple of Jesus Christ.

Jesus has jumped into your boat! You are to be a missionary disciple of Jesus Christ and accompany others closer to God and the Church. Still, perhaps you share Peter's concern and do not think you will "catch anyone in your nets."

When I interact with others about God's call to live as missionary disciples, I often perceive that people are afraid to take on this mission. I heard a priest describe two types of fear that people may experience when they understand that Jesus calls them to be missionary disciples.

Some fear having to give up what is comfortable in their lives. They think that if they live as missionary disciples, they will need to do something they have not done before, such as sharing their faith, praying with others, or spending time with others focused on God. This type of fear stems from the realization that they will have to leave behind a life primarily focused on their needs. As one person put it to me, "I am too busy with things going on in my life to be a missionary disciple."

The second type of fear comes from anxiety about how others will respond. Some worry that others may think negatively of them, tease them, reject their message, or not want to be their friend/family member any longer. They are concerned that others may be "offended" or "upset." I have heard Catholics say such things as, "I don't want to talk about faith with my (adult) children because I'm afraid they will never want to talk with me again," or "I don't talk about the Church because I will not know what to say if I'm asked a question and will look foolish." Some comment, "I just don't know how to begin."

Allow me to bring up one more reason why people do not respond to Jesus' call to be missionary disciples: they are lazy or just don't care. I know this sounds harsh, but for some folks, Jesus has jumped into their boat, and they do not want to be bothered. Now, if you have read this book to this point, I bet you do not fall into this category, still some of the fears I described above may be something that you struggle with.

If fear is keeping you from living as a missionary disciple, remember what Jesus said to Peter in the Gospel passage from Luke: "Do not be afraid." Jesus is in your boat and is with you on your missionary journey. He feeds you with his Body, forgives you through the Sacrament of Reconciliation, and teaches you with his Word. And always remember, Jesus is with you. Especially remember that, where two or more gather in his name, he is with them — a good reason to go on mission two-by-two as described in the Gospels.[26]

Jesus will guide you with the virtue of fortitude that, "ensures firmness in difficulties and constancy in the pursuit of the good."[27] Fortitude gives you the courage to conquer fear so that you can live as a missionary disciple. Fortitude is a gift from God so that you can engage in the life of a baptized priest, prophet, and king. This mission requires time in prayer, discernment of the call, and preparation for the ministry. But remember, you are not doing this

---

[26] See Luke 10:1 and Mark 6:1
[27] *Catechism of the Catholic Church*, 1808

on your own. You are part of Holy Mother Church, and Jesus is with us.

Jesus did not jump into your boat to give you a job, but to offer to you a ministry of love. When you share the name of Jesus, your belief in God, or your life in the Catholic Church, you are talking with others about God, who "is love" (1 John 4:16). When you treat others with kindness, show patience to others, or turn the other cheek, you are reflecting an image of God who "is love." Do not be afraid of living this ministry of love.

Do not fear that living as a missionary disciple is going to take away from your life. Rather, **living this ministry will fulfill it**. To believe this, all you have to do is listen to the Church and the saints to learn that you will flourish to the extent you give yourself as a gift to others. Here are some quotes that drive home this point:

> "[Man] cannot fully find himself except through a sincere gift of himself."[28]

> "[M]an realizes himself through the authentic gift of self."[29]

---

[28] *Gaudium et Spes, 24*
[29] St. Pope John Paul II, 2006, 59:2

"[Y]our being increases and is enhanced in the measure that you give it away."[30]

This is the teaching that St. John Paul II called *The Law of the Gift,* and this is what Jesus asks of you as he sits in your boat. He wants you to "push out into the deep" and be his missionary disciples, to foster holiness as you bring others to Jesus, to speak the name of God to others, and align your part of the world to the truth of the Gospel. Do not be afraid to follow the missionary impulse that the Holy Spirit has placed in your hearts, for Jesus is at your side.

---

[30] Barron, 2008

Prayer

Heavenly Father, pour forth your Holy Spirit. Stir in my soul the desire to renew my faith and deepen my relationship with your Son, our Lord Jesus Christ, so that I might truly believe in and live the Good News. Open my heart to hear the Gospel and grant me the confidence to proclaim the Good News to others. Pour out your Spirit, so that I might be strengthened to go forth and witness to the Gospel in my everyday life through my words and actions.

USCCB
Prayer for the
New Evangelization

Final Reflection Questions

You have reached the end of this book but not the end of your ministry. To prepare to live in a new way as a missionary disciple of Jesus Christ, consider these reflection questions.

<u>For those who are part of a small group book read:</u>
Share with the group one or two new ways you wish to live as a missionary disciple.
How will you pray about the mission?
How will you discern the mission?
How will you prepare for the mission?
How will you begin to accompany others in this mission?
Are there people in this group who are called to the same mission? How can you go out two-by-two (or as a group of three, four, or more) to fulfill the mission?

After talking about these questions, turn to Appendix C and fill out answers to the questions to help prepare you to take missionary action.

<u>For those who read this book on your own:</u>
Go through the questions above and fill out Appendix C, and then share your thoughts with a family member, a Catholic friend, or perhaps a priest or deacon.

REFERENCES

Balke, Bishop Victor (2021). As quoted in "The Perfect Fit: Diocese of Crookston and Sisters of Saint Benedict announce strategic partnership to further shared mission." *Our Northland Diocese*, July, 2021.

Barron, Bishop Robert (2008). *Word on Fire: Proclaiming the Power of Christ*. New York: Crossroad Publishing.

Barron, Bishop Robert (2014). *Priest, Prophet, King* (DVD) Word on Fire.

Catholic Church. (1995). *Catechism of the Catholic Church*. New York: Image Books.

Francis (2013). *The Joy of the Gospel (Evangelii Gaudium)*. Boston: Pauline Books & Media.

John Paul II (2006). *Man and Woman He Created Them: A Theology of the Body*. Boston: Pauline Books & Media.

Rutledge, F. (2015). *The Crucifixion: Understanding the Death of Jesus Christ*. Grand Rapids, MI: Wm. B. Eerdmans.

Twenge, J. M. (2017). *iGen: Why Today's Super-Connected Kids Are Growing Up Less Rebellious, More Tolerant, Less Happy—and Completely Unprepared for Adulthood*. New York: Atria Books.

Vatican Council II. (1975) *Apostolicam Actuositatem, Gaudium et Spes & Lumen Gentium* (documents referenced in this text). In *Documents of Vatican II* edited by Austin P. Flannery OP. Grand Rapids MI: Jove Publications.

APPENDIX A

Resources for Growing as a Missionary Disciple

There are many wonderful resources designed to assist the lay faithful as they grow as missionary disciples of Jesus Christ. The list below is a sample of what is available.

Diocese of Crookston:

Prayers, Bible studies, and other formation resources can be found at: https://www.crookston.org/offices/discipleship/gfad. One specific resource is a book of daily prayer called *31 Prayers for Missionary Disciples,* which can be downloaded for free from: https://www.crookston.org/documents/ministriesoffices/discipleship/2750-31-prayers-for-missionary-disciples/file

Bible studies on missionary discipleship can be found at: https://www.crookston.org/offices/discipleship/gfad/fourpillars/pray

Pope Francis

The Joy of the Gospel, Apostolic Exhortation available at the Vatican Web Site or in a book format.

United States Conference of Catholic Bishops

Living As Missionary Disciples. This brief text explains the vision on missionary discipleship from the USCCB, and it is accessible for free (along with other resources) at: https://www.usccb.org/beliefs-and-teachings/how-we-teach/catechesis/catechetical-sunday/living-disciples

United States Catholic Catechism for Adults (2006) can be found online at: https://www.usccb.org/beliefs-and-teachings/what-we-believe/catechism/us-catholic-catechism-for-adults

Bishop Robert Barron

Through his Word on Fire and YouTube ministries, Bishop Barron has several resources on our baptismal call to be "Priest, Prophet, and King." You can access these at youtube.com or at wordonfire.org. For example, he has a complete DVD collection containing his breakdown of this three-fold ministry in which we are called to participate.

You may also want to look at some of Bishop Barron's books:

To Light a Fire on the Earth

Renewing Our Hope: Essays for the New Evangelization

Redeeming the Time: Gospel Perspectives on the Challenges of the Hour

Stanz, Julianne

Start with Jesus: How everyday disciples will renew the Church. Chicago: Loyola Press. For an excellent comparison of Discipleship and Missionary Discipleship see: https://bit.ly/3PQUnBr

You can also access Juliane Stanz's free online course on missionary discipleship, along with additional online resources at: https://reviveparishes.com/.

Sherry Weddell

You may wish to read through her series of books:

Forming Intentional Disciples

Fruitful Discipleship

Becoming a Parish of Intentional Disciples

Curtis Martin

In his book, *Making Missionary Disciples*, Curtis Martin applies the model used in FOCUS Catholic Campus ministries for Catholics in all situations.

APPENDIX B
Options for Missionary Disciples

*"I dream of a **'missionary option'**—that is, a missionary impulse capable of transforming everything...."*
Pope Francis, *The Joy of the Gospel*

A reflection on possible ways that God is calling you to missionary action.

Review the various missionary options and place a "✓" next to the things you already do; then place a "+" by one to three ideas that you may also be called to do.

Personal Witness

Prayer for Witness:

"Lord, how do you want me to be Your witness in the world?"

-Be cheerful in all your interactions with others — smile!

-When being attended to by someone in a business who is wearing a name tag, thank them by name for their assistance.

-"Turn the other cheek" when wronged by others and treat them with kindness and mercy in return.

-Be a listening ear to those in need of one.

-Accompany through your presence and patience those who struggle in their faith in God and/or the Church.

-Forgive others and ask for their forgiveness.

-When feeling angry or frustrated, pray the "Our Father" or "Hail Mary" and calm down.

-Willingly listen to the faith, life, or relationship struggles that others wish to share.

-Be ever mindful that you are called to be a reflection of God's love in the world.

-Be humbly proud of being a Catholic. Live your life with holy boldness.

-Focus on what is truly important. Relationships are what's important. Christian values are important.

-Participate in a Catholic or ecumenical Bible study or faith sharing group.

-Ask someone to watch a movie or participate in cultural or artistic activities that have healthy spiritual messages.

-Say grace before meals when in public . . . making the Sign of the Cross.

-Place religious statuary in your yard.

-Genuinely use phrases that recognize and give thanks to God: for example, "Thank God," or "God willing."

Proclamation by Word

<u>Prayer for Proclamation:</u>
"Lord, how would you like me to share Your Word with others?"

-Share one of your faith stories with another person.

-Describe how the Church enriches your life.

-Share which phrase or story from the Bible gives you meaning for your life.

-Offer to pray *with* someone.

-Offer to pray *for* someone, and ask them if they have something they would like you to pray about.

-Share with a coworker, neighbor, friend, or parishioner an insight you gained from Sunday Mass.

-Ask someone to share their belief in God with you.

-Offer to share one reason why you choose to believe in God.

-After you get to know someone at a personal level, and they are not attending the Mass, ask them if they would like to join you/your family for Mass.

-Recognize where God has "broken in." Tell others about a recent "God moment."

-Say phrases like, "Thank God," "I believe," or "Amen," in public.

-Wear a crucifix or blessed medal. Say a brief prayer before you put it on.

-Gently challenge an atheist. Ask him/her about their life's purpose. Explain how knowing, loving, praising, and serving God in this life and being happy with Him forever in eternity is your purpose in your Christian life.

-Read about the saints. Share the saint of the day. Tell their stories.

-When you find a good online video or posting that you found helpful for your faith, share it with others.

-Invite someone to join a Bible study with you.

Works of Charity

<u>Prayer for Charity:</u>
"Lord, how would you like me to be more generous with all the gifts You have given me?"

Participate in one or more of the Corporal Works of Mercy. Become involved in efforts to:

-Feed the Hungry: e.g., prepare a meal for a family or person in need.

-Give Drink to the Thirsty: e.g., donate bottled water to a local homeless shelter.

-Shelter the Homeless: e.g., bring gently worn clothing to a local homeless shelter.

-Visit the Sick: e.g., volunteer at a local nursing home or visit the homebound.

-Visit the Prisoners: e.g., collect gifts for children with a parent in prison.

   -Bury the Dead: e.g., visit a local cemetery and pray for the dead.

   -Give alms to the Poor: e.g., find a charity and volunteer to work with the poor.

Remember: Live as a disciple of Jesus Christ, not simply a volunteer! Carry out these works of mercy to reflect God's love and draw others closer to God.

Prayer

<u>Prayer for Guidance</u>
"Lord, how can I pray for others so that they will grow closer to you?"

- Pray for Catholics so that they may grow deeper in their relationship with Jesus Christ.

- Pray for those who were baptized, and/or confirmed Catholic, but no longer attend Church.

-Pray for former Catholics who no longer believe in the Church.

-Pray for former Catholics who no longer believe in God.

-Pray for former Christians who no longer believe in God.

-Pray for family members who no longer attend Mass or no longer believe in God.

-Pray for former parishioners from your parish who have left the Church.

-Pray for God's inspiration for yourself that you may grow deeper in your relationship with Christ, his son, and be inspired by the Holy Spirit to share the Gospel with others.

-Pray a Rosary in public, perhaps while out walking, not to be boastful, but to witness your love of prayer.

-Pray for the souls in Purgatory, particularly deceased loved ones.

-Pray for and support pro-life agencies and organizations.

-Attend a retreat (e.g., Cursillo, Marriage Encounter, etc.) to pray for strength and guidance for the work of evangelizing discipleship.

-Add, or join, a prayer chain in your faith community.

-Spend time reflecting on how the Word of God is calling you to live as a missionary disciple this day, this week, this month, this year. Set a goal to pray daily for at least fifteen minutes, and preferably thirty minutes or more.

Community

<u>Prayer for Wisdom</u>
"Lord, how can I reflect your love in my home and community?"

-Ask a former Catholic why they no longer attend Mass. Listen and ask them questions, and do not become defensive or offended by their statements.

-Invite people into your home, share a meal, and discuss how God has touched lives.

-As you live your life, do as Pope Francis suggests—smile to reflect the Joy of the Gospel.

-Invite people into your home and take part in prayer, such as a Rosary or a Lectio Divina.

-Say please and thank you to everyone in your community as an expression of Christian gratitude.

-Offer to go with someone to priest, deacon, or others when they have a question/concern that you do not know how to address.

-Invite someone to share their story with you; if faith comes up, listen to what they have to say.

-Be bold enough to say, "That is against my faith." Or you can also use "My faith teaches . . ." phrases.

-Be courteous to everyone you meet, especially when they may not be courteous toward you. "Turn the other cheek."

-Show love to your family, have patience in your interactions, express joy in your conversations; and take the time to be with them.

Worship

<u>Prayer for Perseverance:</u>
"Lord, give me strength to persevere in my prayer life and in my worship of you.

-In prayer before Sunday Mass, ask the Holy Spirit to, through this Mass, deepen your commitment to being a missionary disciple.

-Sit in different areas of the Church during Sunday Mass in order to connect with others and make sure to notice the stranger in your midst and talk with them after Mass.

-Attend Mass one additional time each week to pray for the evangelization of the parish, former Catholics, and/or those who do not know God.

-Participate in the Sacrament of Reconciliation (confession) at least once a month. You not only benefit from the sacrament, but you witness your faith in God's mercy.

APPENDIX C
Personal Missionary Discipleship Ministry

I commit to accompany

_____

(List the person or group you will accompany)

Prayer: How will your prayer support this ministry?

Discern: How have you discerned this ministry and what do you need to do to continue the discernment?

Prepare: What do you need to do to prepare you for this accompaniment ministry?

Beyond the three things listed, what is the first thing you need to do to begin this accompaniment ministry?

About the Author

Deacon Mark Krejci and his wife Julie have been married for over 38 years. They have two adult children, who are both married, and two grandchildren. Deacon Mark was ordained as a permanent deacon in 2017, and he is the Director of the Office of Formation in Discipleship and the Director of Deacon Personnel and Formation for the Diocese of Crookston. He earned his PhD from the University of Notre Dame in Counseling Psychology and is a Professor of Psychology at Concordia College in Moorhead, Minnesota.

About *Going Forth As Disciples*

Going Forth As Disciples is a parish-based formation ministry meant to help all Catholics discern how God is calling them to live as missionary disciples. Pope Francis, in the *Joy of the Gospel*, writes "In virtue of their baptism, all the members of the People of God have become Missionary Disciples." Therefore, all Catholics are called to pray and discern God's call as they prepare themselves to accompany others into a closer relationship with God and the Church.

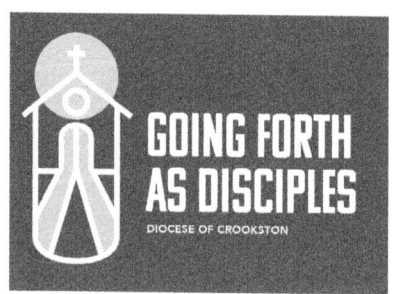

Made in the USA
Monee, IL
17 November 2022